THE NATURAL L/ OF VIOLENCE

By
Michael Edmund Nolan

ISBN: 979-8-7885-6565-1

DISCLAIMER

The views expressed in this publication are those of the author and do not necessarily reflect the official policy or position of the Department of Defense or the U.S. government. The public release clearance of this publication by the Department of Defense does not imply Department of Defense endorsement or factual accuracy of the material.

Front Cover Photo: Ambush in Mosul, Iraq, 2004. Author's collection.

This book is dedicated to the Goddess of War in all of Her guises. May she ever and always guide my spear into the heart of my enemy.

Acknowledgments

I would like to sincerely thank my wife, Erin, for all of her patience and devotion as well as her time in editing this book. Thanks also goes out to my friend and fellow soldier, Christian Rathvon Herring, for reviewing earlier drafts and offering up insightful advice, guidance, and thoughts.

Preface

I am not a Navy SEAL. I am not U.S. Army Special Forces. I am not Marine Corps Force Recon. I am a former Marine infantryman who, after his initial tour in the Marine Corps, served a couple of years in the Marine Corps Reserves before eventually switching over to the Army National Guard. In total, I served over 24 years as an enlisted service member and my perspective on things is simply that of an average Joe. There are so many books written by senior officers that not only discuss their experiences but also provide insight and analysis of their observations within the framework of modern military thought. The vast majority of books written by my fellow enlisted service members, however, typically tell the story of their military adventures, great as they may be, but usually make no attempt to come to unique conclusions about military strategy or doctrine. This book attempts to break that pattern.

Within these pages you will find what a basic infantryman who spent 19 years operating at the platoon level, 'in the trenches,' has to offer modern military thought. Having participated in several military campaigns in various continents, I have a tremendous amount of tactical experience. That experience was then distilled during my final years of service as an infantry instructor into a body of knowledge concerning the nature of war and violence. It should be noted, however, that these observations are coming from someone devoted to the martial arts. As such, they include a conscious effort to go beyond mere war and violence. The hope is that those who have also been called to a life of military service will see opportunities in their vocation for personal growth and development like no other. And for those who rightly hate all things pertaining to war, the hope is that this book will provide an understanding of the mechanics of violence needed to effectively grow the peace. Just as a doctor cannot be expected to treat an illness with no knowledge of the workings of disease, so too is it impossible for the advocates of stability and diplomacy to work their magic if they know nothing of the workings of war.

Table of Contents

The Study of Dark Things
Page 1

The Natural Laws of Violence
Page 18

The Money Men
Page 37

The Aluminum Level of Leadership
Page 56

The Effects of Exposure
Page 72

The Study of Dark Things

It is important to start with a story. One that I like to tell comes from my time as an infantry instructor. I would say to my students, imagine two boys where one is poor but large and strong, and one is rich but only of average size and strength. The rich boy has his lunch money every day, but the poor boy never has anything. In this scenario the poor boy comes over to the rich boy and says, "If you don't give me your lunch money, I'm going to hurt you." The rich boy, out of fear, gives the poor boy, a real bully, all of his money.

Now imagine a second scenario with the exact same set up – one large and strong poor boy with nothing and one average sized rich boy with everything. In the second scenario, however, the rich boy happens to be a 10th degree ninja and when the poor boy, the bully, comes over and says, "If you don't give me your lunch money, I'm going to hurt you," the rich boy says nothing. The poor boy then attempts to take the money by force but the rich boy is not only able to defend himself, but he manages to subdue the bully with a choke hold, render him unconscious, and even bind his hands before the bully awakens. Once the poor boy regains consciousness, the rich boy tells him, "Even though you have behaved dishonorably, I will share with you some of my money so that we both can eat." The poor boy agrees and so it is done.

Having been presented with these two scenarios, the first question I would then ask my students was, "In which scenario does the poor boy have the opportunity to be generous?" Even though this never seemed to be a controversial question, (God bless my students) they would often struggle to think about how the poor boy, who had nothing, could have been generous, never really arriving at a satisfactory option. A common suggestion would be for the poor boy, at least in scenario one, to offer his protection in exchange for some money. In response I would ask 1) since when did the exchange of services for money, aka a standard business transaction, become an act of generosity, and 2) does this mean that the protection rackets set up by mobsters against local small businesses actually amount to great acts of generosity!? The group would typically acknowledge that one has to possess something of some value that they are then able to give away in order to be generous.

I would then ask my students, "In which scenario is the rich boy actually generous?" Unanimously and without exception my classes would state that only in the second scenario was the rich boy generous. I would then point out the obvious – that in both scenarios the rich boy gave money to the poor boy but that only in the first scenario did he give the poor boy all of it. The response from my students typically involved what you, the reader here and now, probably finds to be true as well. The giving in the first scenario stemmed from fear and was forced and therefore devoid of free will. To which I would typically concede but point out that when one considers that free will appears to be an acknowledged prerequisite to generosity, it is noteworthy that the poor boy was powerful enough in the first scenario to take this free will and in the second scenario the rich boy was powerful enough to defend it. This suggests that some degree of power is also required to be generous.

By this point, half my students would be bored and falling asleep but the other half – I would even go so far as to say the smarter half – would start getting a bit agitated. This suggestion that both power and abundance of some sort are required to be generous simply bothered them. It seemed to them immoral somehow. I even had one incredibly sharp student recount a story he had heard regarding two prisoners of war. One had no food and the other merely scraps and yet the one with the scraps shared what he had with the other prisoner and the student claimed that neither were in a position of power nor had any abundance and yet there was certainly an act of generosity.

For those who have spent even just a modest amount of time studying the particularly dark subject of torture, its mechanisms, and its various effects would be aware that, in fact, these prisoners retained a degree of both power and abundance. Not only could the scraps be seized and what little remained of their freedom be taken, but even their ability to think and act can be destroyed. Admittedly, taking things to such an extreme often results in death, but the point remains that it can be done. That is not to say that this story of the prisoners given in response to the rich boy/poor boy scenarios has no value in redefining the claim that generosity can only occur when one is in a position of both power and abundance. The story of the prisoners makes it clear that such a claim can only be true if one defines both power and abundance in the broadest of terms. And to that I certainly agree.

The question, however, remains, 'what does this have to do with violence?' Is the point merely that violence can be used to do bad things. If so, thanks for nothing there, Captain Obvious. No, the point is actually to initiate thought and discussion regarding a multitude of variables surrounding life and organic systems and how they interplay. Not only are power, abundance, necessities (e.g., food), and violence things to be considered, but so too are their opposites of weakness, scarcity, wants, and peace. The scenarios above provide the building blocks for a mental exercise involving the synthesis of specific variables that one can use to develop models of the general system.[1] They represent the kind of critical thinking that true warriors use to develop themselves and improve their ability to effect strategic impacts. And, although I do sincerely care about my brothers and sisters-in-arms and the degree of their professionalism and expertise as Marines, Soldiers, Sailors, or Airmen, I care more about them as human beings. As such, this leads me to suggest that the study of violence, warfare, and military science in general should be pursued with a desire for not just professional development, but personal development as well.

In China, a classical education typically entails the study of Confucianism as well as five specific subjects, sometimes referred to as the five excellencies, which are thought to be connected in the form of a circle that describes the processes of nature. The five subjects are medicine (life), music, art, poetry, and martial arts (death). It is thought that none of the five subjects can truly be mastered without studying all the others at least to some degree. There is a common story told to aspirants specifically in the martial arts traditions to drive this notion home.

Not too long ago there were two martial artists named Kim and Lee. Kim and Lee were boyhood friends but once they became adults, each had decided to go to a different temple to devote their lives to studying Buddhism and the martial arts. After many decades, their paths crossed near a lake and Lee was so excited to see Kim that he couldn't wait to show Kim the skills that he had developed during his training. Almost immediately, he ran out onto the lake to show Kim that he could actually walk on water. Kim praised his accomplishments but walked over to a boatman nearby whom he paid $2 to ferry him across the lake. Lee asked Kim, "What are you doing? Why are you leaving? Did you not also develop such skills at your temple?" Kim replied that he was merely trying to show Lee that he had wasted his decades of training at the temple to learn what amounted to a $2 skill.

The idea here being that a martial artist who only works to develop his skills as a warrior is just developing a cheap skill. What is the cost of ammunition these days? The ability to kill at will is basically only worth the price of a bullet. So why do Shaolin Monks, Buddhist clergy forbidden to kill, devote so much of their time to practicing the martial arts if mastery of those arts is of such little value? It is because violence and warfare are governed by natural laws that care nothing about the opinion of any human being. Therefore, it serves as a great tool to put one's ego in check and to train one's mind to focus on what is truly known in the here and now. On the field of battle, reliance on opinion and assumptions is fatal. And it is precisely this forcing function towards rationality and objectivity that allows the profession of arms to simultaneously serve as a vocation and a path towards personal development.

But before we fall too madly in love with rationality and objectivity and the benefits derived therefrom, let us examine briefly if that is all that the study of violence and warfare brings us. The profession of arms, like the profession of medicine, is a practitioners art governed by the laws of nature. We see that if a medical doctor, as a scientific professional, were to correctly apply the scientific method they have been formally trained in for years, often they would be forced to use language that reflects an acknowledgement that other possibilities exist when the limits of rationality and objectivity have been reached. This would result in language that is inconclusive but accurate. Examples of such language include, "It appears that you likely have cancer," or, "The test results suggest that your symptoms are a result of…" or, "I think that the best course of action may be to…" But to a patient such language sounds very uncertain and undecisive. Not surprisingly, many patients when presented with such language are eager to find a second 'opinion' from a doctor who is more confident and who actually 'knows' what is going on even though a doctor who uses such language is actually being more scientifically accurate.

Successfully dealing with the uncertainties that lie beyond the bounds of reason and logic is a must for the practitioners of both medicine and war. Reason and logic are a necessary prerequisite because they define where the valid questions regarding the unknown begin but they remain just a prerequisite. To use a ridiculously extreme example, say one is debating about the possible sources of the universe's creation and they are presented with two options. Option one suggests that a creative force of some sort led to the creation of the universe. Option two suggests that flying monkeys which issue forth from one's butt created the universe. Option two is not valid. Reason and logic dictate that flying monkeys in the universe may not exist, and, even if they do, there are certainly and irrefutably no flying monkeys that issue forth from one's butt. As vague and ill-defined as it may be, only option one remains as a valid possibility within the realm of the unknown because only option one remains within the bounds of possibility defined by reason and logic.

Think of reason and logic, rationality and objectivity, as the straight lines of the known that define the circle boundary of the valid unknowns within which practitioners are forced to operate. To a modern warrior this image should be eerily similar to what is seen looking through the rifled barrel of a gun. In the next chapter, we will explore the masculine, straight-line, and rational approach to defining violence and warfare. This essentially defines the straight lines. In chapter three, we will then explore the feminine, circular, and intuitive aspects of violence and warfare that show us the proper attitude to have to successfully achieve results when dealing with the unknown. Finally, in the last two chapters, insights on leadership and military service in general will be provided merely as examples of the application of this dualistic view of war.

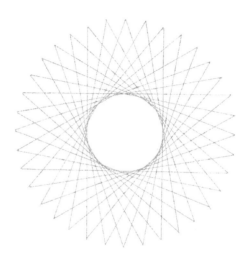

<u>Chapter Notes</u>

[1] If all you know about Col John Boyd is his OODA Loop theory, choke yourself! Then go find his paper on the

internet entitled, *Destruction and Creation*, dated 03 September 1976 and read it immediately.

The Natural Laws of Violence

How do we define violence? What does it look like? The classical Principles of War espoused by the United States found in the old American Army Field Manual 3-0, *Operations*, are tools used to educate and guide officers in the planning of operations and strategy. However, they are not absolute. For example, the principle of Mass can on the one hand generate overwhelming force against the enemy, but on the other hand it can create nothing more than a choice target for the enemy allowing them to achieve a decisive victory. Or take the principle of Surprise. Surprise can be an effects multiplier of shocking magnitude, or it can turn into nothing more than a rush to failure. What makes the difference then between success and failure if one is genuinely applying these so-called principles of war?!

I cannot say it enough. War is violence, albeit on a large scale, and as such is governed by the natural laws of violence. The principles of war are meant to be guidelines for planning purposes. The successful application of these guidelines, however, is dependent upon the extent to which the planner uses the principles of war in accordance with the natural laws that govern violence. Perhaps not surprisingly then it has always shocked me that these natural laws of violence have not been articulated in doctrine like the principles of war.

This may be because natural laws are difficult to pin down. Just look at physics. There are a boat load of hypotheses and a whole host of theorems out there, but, even after decades, if not centuries, of research by the brightest minds in human history there really are not that many actual laws in all of physics (e.g., laws of motion, light, and gravity/relativity to name a few). Natural laws such as these are irrefutable because they are completely testable by scientific standards. These standards demand such things as replicability of laboratory results demonstrating the absolute nature of a law.

With such a high standard to legitimately claim the irrefutability of something, it becomes a bit more reasonable to try something else instead – like outlining general principles describing ways to use the effects of such laws to one's advantage. That is what the principles of war are all about. However, I believe there is tremendous value in attempting to identify the natural laws of violence using the laboratory of hand-to-hand combat. Just as we have seen the fruit produced from the tree of knowledge regarding physics and the application of the natural laws identified therein to such areas as energy (e.g., nuclear power) and communications (e.g., fiber optics), so too would the professional warrior gain tremendously from a greater knowledge of the natural laws governing violence and an understanding of how the principles of war flow from them. You find some of this approach among the Asian masters such as Sun Tzu. Yet, ideas from western writers on the subject do not appear to have stuck nor, I would argue, has anyone in the west effectively outlined the place and utility for such concepts within contemporary military doctrine.

So, in order to jump start the

discussion on this, below I am proposing some natural laws of violence that I have observed over the course of my various combat deployments and throughout my life as a dedicated martial artist. These are meant to be nothing more than a starting point. I readily acknowledge that some may, in time, be found unworthy of the title 'natural law.' I invite others to contribute their observations of what they believe to be some of the natural laws governing violence. It is my sincerest hope that eventually military doctrine will successfully identify all of the laws in order to better train its officers and NCOs in the use of the principles of war in their planning and execution of military operations.

Nolan's First Natural Law of Violence: The first participant to effectively use violence will be victorious.

The devil is in the details on this first law. It is easiest to explain with an example. Suppose one man punches another man unexpectedly, using the so-called and much beloved 'sucker punch.' Assuming the punch was truly effective, the aggressor in this case, who was the first person to effectively use violence against his opponent, will be victorious. The key words here being 'first' and 'effective.'

Now, suppose the target of the sucker punch was not caught unaware and he manages to pull out a gun. Because the gun is more effective than a fighter's bare hands, if the gunslinger were to use it effectively against his opponent before the opponent could effectively use his hands, the gunslinger would win. He would win because he was the first pugilist to effectively use violence even though his opponent was clearly ready and about to use a level of violence himself. The key elements of this first law, namely TIMELINESS (being first) and EFFECTIVENESS, in turn lead to the next two laws.

Nolan's Second Natural Law of Violence: Violence naturally tends to escalate.

This second law flows directly from the timeliness and effectiveness aspects of the first law. It is obvious that if being the first to effectively use violence is what is needed to guarantee victory, then participants in violence will naturally strive after the most effective means of executing violence at their disposal and will attempt to do so as quickly as possible - particularly if they are unable to effectively use the current level of violence to secure that victory. I purposely use the phrase "tend to" to soften the language of this law because there are exceptions. Particularly, when you have one participant that is significantly stronger than the other. In the face of the futility of any violent engagement (see the Fourth Natural Law), the weaker participant will often refuse to engage and simply accept the damage done by the more powerful participant to minimize the likelihood of ESCALATION, the key element in this second law.

Nolan's Third Natural Law of Violence: Action is required to be victorious in violent situations.

This third law merely recognizes that the need to be effective – to achieve effects on target – as outlined in the first law naturally demands that an action must be taken for one to be victorious in a violent situation. This is exactly where Col Boyd's famous OODA loop comes into play.[2] It is extremely important, however, to define and understand the key element of ACTION found in this law in the broadest of terms. What do I mean by this?

By way of example, I recently had the honor of attending a Brazilian Jiu Jitsu seminar with one of the most senior American practitioners of the art. He relayed a terrific story about a wrestling opponent who got upset that the match was going nowhere, and that the American grandmaster appeared to be doing nothing. The grandmaster asked his opponent, "Are you choking me right now?" The opponent said, "No." The grandmaster asked, "Do you have me in any kind of a joint lock or submission hold?" The opponent said again, "No," to which the grandmaster replied, "Then I am absolutely doing something." In this case the grandmaster was allowing his opponent, a younger and stronger practitioner, to expend more energy than the grandmaster in the opponent's efforts 'to do something.' Over time this energy expenditure would ultimately negate the younger opponent's superior strength and allow the grandmaster to easily subdue his opponent once the balance of physical power had tipped in the grandmaster's favor. The point is that action must be present in order to achieve victory though it can be extremely subtle.

Nolan's Fourth Natural Law of Violence: The ideal position for a participant is one where the participant can effectively execute violence against others, but others cannot effectively execute violence against the participant.

Probably a classic image one could use to capture this law would be that of an adult holding a child at bay by stiff arming the child on their forehead. The adult can clearly strike the child and yet the child is powerless to strike the adult in any meaningful way. Although that is just a silly example, it demonstrates the point of this fourth law very well. Another example would be one participant behind a protective barrier with a weapon that can reach 1,000 meters engaging another unprotected participant, who is out in the open at a distance of 800 meters and possesses a weapon that can only reach 500 meters. That is the ideal position for the first participant. The key element here is POSITIONING.

It should be noted that because there are so many variables at play, true combat is multi-dimensional and opportunities to assume such ideal positioning are admittedly rare. Even when manufactured by a skilled warrior, ideal positioning will typically only exist at a specific place during a specific time after which it evaporates. The advantages gained by superior positioning, however, are incredibly profound because they leverage several of the other key elements, including timeliness, effectiveness, and action. Accordingly, failure to take advantage of opportunities for superior positioning is tantamount to a sin against nature and will only serve to accelerate one's defeat.

Now let us use these key elements of timeliness, effectiveness, escalation, action, and positioning to analyze first a traditional American Principle of War and then a Russian Principle of Military Art. Let us start with Economy of Force that the Americans define as the need to, "Expend minimum essential combat power on secondary efforts to allocate the maximum possible combat power on primary efforts." The emphasis here is on effectiveness and the main point is to focus action on where it will be most effective. But the proper use of Economy of Force also leverages timeliness and positioning. By conserving resources as much as possible, one is better able to take advantage of opportunities for superior positioning when they occur than a participant who has not conserved their resources. This superior positioning, in turn, allows one to initiate violence and even escalate matters in a way that is significantly detrimental to one's opponent.

Conversely, the key elements also highlight ways in which a Principle of War such as Economy of Force can be misapplied. Keeping with the emphasis on effectiveness, should the combat power applied to primary efforts be ineffective, it matters little if the bulk of this power is being applied to those efforts. Far from being an example of efficiency, it amounts to a waste of resources. Similarly, should an entity never get around to taking crucial action in the hopes of maintaining Economy of Force, whatever efficiencies one might achieve will be for naught, which is actually addressed in the second part of the American Principle that directs one "to allocate the maximum combat power on primary efforts."

Finally, let us close with a look at the Russian Principle of Reflexive

Control. The Russians define this principle as "providing a stimulus (information, an action, etc.) to make an opponent do something for himself (organize in a specific way, develop certain weaponry, maneuver, etc.) that he is doing for the initiator of the action."[3] This is something that is regularly used in hand-to-hand combat and is one of the most important concepts for a warrior to understand as they start their journey. This concept relies upon and takes advantage of the instinctive understanding of the natural laws of violence within one's opponent.

As an example of reflexive control, think of a wrestler who grabs the back of his opponent's neck and pushes his opponents head face down hard towards the ground. The natural reaction of most opponents will be, at a minimum, to resist this downward pressure which, of necessity, entails the use of upward pressure to some extent. The moment the wrestler feels the initiation of this upward pressure, he immediately deploys a set of techniques that depend on an upward motion by his opponent and can range from anything like a sumo throat/face push upwards and backwards to a leg takedown of some sort. The main point is that the wrestler intentionally elicited a specific response from the opponent and that response was designed to actually support the follow-on technique of the wrestler.

Reflexive control is a form of action that is designed to provide superior positioning, which in turn can be leveraged to create more effective outcomes on the target than could be had otherwise. In doing so, it usually precludes effective action on the part of one's opponent, thereby often granting one the advantages of first strike (timeliness) as well. The natural laws of violence also highlight how reflexive control can be misapplied. They tell us that, because of the need for timeliness, the initiating stimulus (e.g., the downward pushing on the opponent's neck) must be simple. Imagine a boxer trying to implement this Russian principle by using a seven-punch combination as the initiating stimulus. When such a complex stimulus is used, it becomes nearly impossible to guarantee a specific reaction on the part of one's opponent. Furthermore, as that stimulus drags on, the likelihood that the opponent will choose to simply escalate matters in a manner that better suites their comparative advantages increases dramatically.

I invite the reader to perform this sort of intellectual consideration using the proposed natural laws of violence on any other such principle of war cited by any country's military. This attempt at defining known mechanisms of violence concludes our exploration of the masculine, straight-line, and rational approach to defining violence and warfare. Now let us explore the feminine, circular, and intuitive aspects of violence and warfare that show us the proper attitude to have to successfully achieve results when dealing with the unknown.

Chapter Notes

[2] For more information see https://en.wikipedia.org/wiki/OODA_loop.

[3] Thomas, Timothy L. (2019, August). *Russian Military Thought: Concepts and Elements*. The MITRE Corporation.

The Money Men

The observations regarding the natural laws of violence may naturally lead one to ask about the human laws of war and their validity – or at the very least their relationship to these natural laws.[4] Obviously natural laws will always trump human laws. No human legislature can pass a law making it illegal for light to shine and expect light obey. Similarly, the natural laws of violence will always trump any human laws regarding the matter. There is, however, a very important observation regarding the relationship between violence and human law that needs to be made. Violence is the very foundation of all human law.

Humans can be quite emotional, but there are at least two emotions, greed and fear, that turn out to be somewhat problematic for group dynamics in a social species such as ours.[5] There is greed for sex and wealth and there is fear of violence. In this discussion, the reader must understand that wealth in this context is synonymous with the associated status that wealth provides. Hence fighting for honor and all other such intangibles really relates back to the perception of wealth and success and the opportunities for sex that those things provide. Humans typically engage in violence with other humans due to some perceived deficiency or imbalance in the distribution of wealth. When it becomes apparent to would be aggressors that the parties involved are mutually capable of killing each other, then there is the needed incentive to come to terms on how wealth is to be divided without violence. Only in such an environment where there is a healthy level of fear that violence will result if agreed to rules are not adhered to are laws born and obeyed. Thus, it is violence that drives law and law that drives behavior simply because of fear of the violence that underlies the law in the first place. This is evidenced by the fact that the penalties for violating the law, even in modern societies, consists of violent acts to be executed against the offender ranging from imprisonment to death.

And though it may appear that this does not apply to civil cases, that would be a false conclusion. Think of a civil judgment where property is awarded to the victor in the case. Should the losing side fail to provide the property, rest assured that folks with guns, commonly referred to as the sheriff, will show up on the loser's doorstep and physically seize the property – violently if needed. So, although civil cases typically do not determine innocence or guilt for violating the peace, and hence no violent punishments may result, should either party feel dissatisfied with the results of a civil trial, and should that party have the power to engage in violence against the other party with impunity, the losing party is free to do so and more than likely will to maintain its wealth as often occurs in many countries. This normally does not occur in the United States only because neither party is ever powerful enough to attack the other with impunity. The criminal statutes against such violence would be enforced against the retaliatory party. So we are brought back, even in civil cases, to the violent realities that underlie all legal systems.

This can be a sad and depressing

observation. But this actually leads to
the real value and incredible genius
behind human law. When one looks at
the earliest human laws, such as the
famous Code of Hammurabi or the
lesser known though older Codes of Ur-
Nammu, although there is certainly
violence committed by the State on
behalf of the aggrieved to limit the
extent of retributional violence, the
amazing contribution of human law is
the monetization of violence. Human
law, even from the earliest days to the
present, abounds with directives
providing compensation in exchange
for harms done. This legal notion of
monetary fines in lieu of violence-as-
payback has done more for human
evolution, in my opinion, than anything
else except the development of
language itself.[6] This can be hard to
see for those of us living in a modern
country where legal systems have

grown quite complex and are often taken for granted. But for those of us who have had the misfortune of traveling in dangerous places where human law has been forsaken and violence reigns supreme, the immense power and incalculable value of such laws becomes readily apparent.

The question remains, however, what does this ancient relationship between money and violence have to do with the feminine aspects of warfare and how one is to deal with uncertainty and the unknown? For this we are brought back to the emotions of fear and greed and the animals of Wall Street lore.[7] Most people are familiar with the bull that strikes upward with its horns and hence the analogy with rising markets as well as the bear that strikes downward with its claws and its association with falling markets. But most people are less familiar with the bull and bear's intended targets, namely the pigs and sheep that embody greed and fear respectively. Unfortunately, it turns out that the marketplace is not as far removed from the battlefield as one might think.

While attending the Eisenhower School (one of the war colleges at National Defense University), one of my instructors relayed a story about an incident involving a Marine Corps flag officer, Lt.Gen. Paul K. Van Riper, who, at the time, thought it would be a good idea to expose Marine officers to the stock market trading pits in New York City.[8] One can only assume the good General met a Wall Street connection at a convention or a cocktail party or something along those lines that eventually led to this situation. I personally have no idea. My war college instructor was not part of the story himself and so he did not know all of the details of the incident, so this is more of a summary of the lesson my instructor tried to convey as opposed to an historic account of a situation that has since taken on increasingly legendary proportions.

As the story goes, upon arrival in New York and after the standard tour and brief introduction to the mechanics of the trading process, the Marine officers were given the chance to trade against the professional traders in a trading simulation pit. Not surprisingly, the professional traders quickly outmatched the Marine officers some of whom supposedly blew their entire accounts – meaning they lost everything. If the story ended there it wouldn't be that big of a deal. The traders were in their element doing what they are the supposed experts at doing. They theoretically should have outperformed the Marines.

It was all a good-natured learning experience and after returning to Quantico the Marines eventually invited the traders to come down from New York to learn about life as a Marine and to participate in a simulated war game. It's only proper, after all, to return the favor and the traders took Lt.Gen. Van Riper (probably a Brigadier General at the time) up on his offer. Much to everyone's surprise, however, the traders were victorious in the war game, the supposed domain of the Marines! Despite leading to a fair amount of embarrassment and shame, to the great credit of my beloved Marine Corps, it also led to a good bit of study and analysis.

It turns out that the traders had developed an amazing ability. The traders were able to assess the environment they found themselves in and put themselves in other people's positions, thereby successfully predicting the likely course of action that other people would take. They would then choose a course of action for themselves that would best enhance their own position, in the markets or in war, based upon this high probability assessment of what others would do. Additionally, because it was such an important element in their professional success and because markets can move almost instantly, the traders developed the ability to perform this decision-making process very quickly.

The important key is the extremely high degree of empathy that allows one to not just effectively put oneself in the shoes of one's opponent, but to define possible courses of action the opponent has available and assign fairly accurate degrees of probability to the various options available to one's opponent. This ability is so very crucial to develop in a warrior because violence, in reality, should be defined as actions taken against a foe in a world of probabilities.[9] Although anything is possible, there is only a very small subset of that infinite list of possibilities that are highly probable. Conversely, virtually nothing is 100% probable and by accepting this definition of violence, the warrior is forced to acknowledge the fact that they do not know everything and can only, at best, assign probabilities to enemy courses of action and move out accordingly, all the while remaining vigilant to the fact that things may not be unfolding as expected.

All of this highlights the need to train to develop this empathy and the ability to work naturally with probabilities. Historically, the Asian martial arts begin the process of this sort of training through what is often referred to as sensitivity training. Examples of this are Tai Chi push-hands training or Wing Chun Chi Sau (sticky hands) training. Eventually, though, a warrior needs to gain an intuitive, 'in the bones,' understanding of statistics and the mathematics behind probabilities. This is best achieved by playing statistics games.

A common introductory game involves a red ball and three cups. The red ball is secretly placed in one of the cups and the student is asked to pick a cup with the goal of choosing the cup containing the red ball. After the student has chosen a cup, one of the two cups not chosen and that does not contain the ball is removed from play. The student is then asked to decide if they want to keep their chosen cup or switch to the last cup remaining before revealing where the red ball has been placed. The game is performed multiple times and the results of both staying put and of switching cups are recorded. In this way, over time, the student realizes that switching cups leads to the greatest chance of success and, more importantly, a personal understanding of why is developed.

Eventually, for those who demonstrate both an interest and the aptitude, active participation in the markets can be attempted. Because of the risk of a gambling addiction, this should be limited to mature individuals and even then, only paper trading should be the norm for the purposes of training. For those who want to explore this further, I recommend a mathematics-based approach, often provided by options trading due to the Black-Scholes model, as a good example of how reason can be applied to what is known about the marketplace and then probabilities used to address what is not fully defined in order for a course of action with a greater chance of success to be identified and pursued.

Now let us apply this dualistic Yin-Yang approach to warfare in two areas, leadership and service, in order to explore and demonstrate the practicality of the approach particularly as we walk the path of the warrior as people striving to better ourselves and not just killers wasting our lives to acquire some $2 skill.

Chapter Notes

[4] As a complete side note, the current U.S. Department of Defense manual on the laws of war dated June of 2015 is garbage. One would be far better served reading these two articles by Rabkin:

1) Rabkin, J. (2015). *Anglo-*

American Dissent From the European Law of War: A History with Contemporary Echoes. San Diego Law Review, 52(1), 1–72.

2) Rabkin, J. (2015). *Proportionality in Perspective: Historical Light on the Law of Armed Conflict*. San Diego International Law Journal, 16(2), 263–340.

Then compare and contrast the current DoD manual with the *Law of Land Warfare*, FM 27-10, dated 18 July 1956, and see for oneself, in light of the natural laws of violence discussed, where things are perhaps starting to go astray.

[5] One can certainly add hatred and a whole host of other negative emotions, but the analysis ends the same.

[6] Lawyers actually did a good

thing for humanity?! Shocker. I know. A more subtle example of how legal structures exist in order to mitigate violence and promote unity involves one of America's greatest strengths – it's cultural diversity. Not only do our open immigration policies assist us with maintaining a healthier labor pyramid where there are a greater number of younger workers supporting the elderly that have retired, but the comparative openness of Americans towards immigrants has created a large reservoir of cultures from which the uniquely American culture has woven its amalgamated tapestry of customs, norms, and traditions. From an American military service member's perspective, one of the advantages of this diversity has been the establishment of government structures from the very founding of the country that ensure not just checks and balances between the branches of government, but more importantly structures that ensure the consideration of minority views. This directly serves to diffuse conflict and preempt the need for revolution, thus sparing the U.S. Military from having to constantly fight a never-ending series of civil wars as is the norm in many countries and regions of the world.

[7] See Jacob, A. (2016). Bulls, bears, chickens and pigs: Why investors use animals to explain the stock market. Yahoo!Finance. https://finance.yahoo.com/news/bulls-bears-chickens-pigs-why-000000860.html for a good but basic breakdown of the associated mythology.

[8] Articles about this incident are hard to find but a good one, if you can find it, that not only summarizes the story but briefly talks about the

implications is Thomas A. Stewart's How to Think With Your Gut originally published in the November 2002 issue of Business 2.0.

[9] The word 'foe' is purposely singular. When asked about fighting multiple opponents at the same time, Morihei Ueshiba, the found of Aikido, was quoted as saying something along the lines of, "When faced with multiple opponents, treat them as one great enemy and fight on." This is indeed the way.

The Aluminum Level of Leadership

The following is a speech, edited for brevity and clarity, that I gave at a commissioning ceremony for three new lieutenants who had just completed the Officer Candidate School (OCS) at the 183rd Regimental Training Institute in Ft. Pickett, Virginia, where I was, at the time, an OCS instructor. The distinguished guests in attendance were Brigadier General Timothy P. Williams, the Adjutant General of the State of Virginia, and Brigadier General Walter L. Mercer, the Land Component Commander of the Virginia National Guard. It highlights a basic approach to leadership in combat and concludes with the need to apply both the masculine (Ares) as well as the feminine (Athena) aspects of leadership in order to achieve true success as a leader.

* * *

Good afternoon, ladies and gentlemen, General Williams, General Mercer, distinguished guests and visitors, family members, and especially the three young men whose accomplishment we are here to honor and celebrate. It did not escape me that a privilege such as this – being the guest speaker at a commissioning ceremony – is not usually given to someone with a rank such as mine. And for that privilege I am truly honored.

Ladies and gentlemen, the Army has put forth a fairly basic model for leadership, which it encapsulates with the phrase, "Be – Know – Do." And although I have absolutely no problem with that model, I have found that sometimes, by virtue of its simplicity, it isn't quite directive enough for some would-be leaders uncertain about how they should go about things. And this is no small issue! U.S. military doctrine claims that there are three levels of leadership: tactical, operational, and strategic. Quite conveniently these match what doctrine claims are the three levels of war. This often leads some to think that there are different kinds of leadership, but there is no such thing. Leadership is leadership is leadership.

I often like to use the example of my time spent learning to be a blacksmith. My father was a fairly prominent farrier, which is a blacksmith that specializes in making horseshoes and horseshoeing. I myself learned the trade at the Oklahoma Horseshoeing School in Purcell, OK, studying under Dr. Jack Roth. When you start out learning to be a blacksmith, you work exclusively with iron and steel. Pretty quickly an apprentice is able to get the hang of it and particularly if he or she is strong or keen eyed, they find that they are able to craft some decent looking horseshoes. That's about the time that the master hands the apprentice a bar of aluminum to work with. Racehorses wear aluminum horseshoes because the metal is so light weight. Well, it is also very soft.

Immediately, with the very first blow of the hammer, the lack of skill in the apprentice is made self-evident. No amount of strength, no fancy set of tools, and no keenness of sight can compensate for a lack of skill as a blacksmith when working with aluminum. The same holds true for leadership in war. At the lowest, or tactical level, when a new lieutenant is leading a platoon of men, like working with iron, he or she can offset a lack of leadership with a strong dose of technical knowledge. At the operational level, a young major can hide their inability to lead by spouting forth doctrine and enforcing the best practices they have observed in others. But things become a bit more difficult for such a field grade officer because more of their job involves and demands actual leadership. And harder still is it for a general grade officer to hide any lack of leadership capability, because their entire job truly does involve the exercise of leadership. The strategic level of war, which is the level at which general grade officers operate, is just like the bar of aluminum that will only take shape at the hands of a skilled blacksmith. Now I apologize, Generals. You may have thought that you operate at the gold or platinum level of war, but I would say it is actually the aluminum level! I'm sorry that I'm the one who had to break the news to you.

All of this matters because I have never been interested in creating new lieutenants. I have made it very clear to both the officer candidates and to my superiors that I am here to create generals and I fully expect at least one of my officer candidates to wear a star on their shoulders someday. And the way that I propose they will get there is by following Sergeant Nolan's model for leading soldiers. It is a very simple three step process. Step one is be the best, step two is set a standard of excellence, and step three is enforce that standard.

Every organization I have ever been in has what I would call its natural leader. Often it is the person at the top, but not always. The natural leader is the person the majority of the team members prefer and typically choose to follow. This person commands more of the respect and confidence of those around them than anyone else. Though a person doesn't have to be the absolute best at everything to earn such respect, my observation has been that a person does have to be very good if not one of the best at most things. A leader needs to be that person that everyone respects because then and only then, when you are among the best, will you have the moral authority in the group to perform step two, set a standard of excellence.

Now one may question the need for a standard of excellence and whether or not that is really a necessity of leadership to which I normally respond with the story of the fat Master Sergeant who lives in the TOC. You see, ladies and gentlemen, over the course of my career I have, on occasion, found myself on patrol engaged with the enemy. And on more than one of these occasions I have had to radio the TOC, the Tactical Operations Center, or simply higher headquarters in more layman's terms, in order to either inform my chain of command about current events or to request assistance. And more than once, the person on the receiving end of these radio transmissions was a fat Master Sergeant. I am not trying to be cruel in my description nor am I trying to be overly pejorative or disrespectful. I am merely describing the facts of the situation.

Without exception, whenever I found myself in those situations, the fat Master Sergeant would get extremely excited about what was going on, which, to be fair, is understandable. However, we are all professionals and, to be frank, I did not have time to deal with what followed. You see, ladies and gentlemen, what followed my initial transmission wasn't the response of, "how can we help," that I expected. No. In one case, it was almost infantile questions about the gory details of events. In the other case, it was a barrage of purely administrative and legalistic questioning such as, "did you obey the rules of engagement," or "did you follow every step outlined in the escalation of force card that you had to sign acknowledging the assumption of responsibility for any and all actions you may take or fail to take as appropriate?" Either way, they were the words of someone whose career in the military had gone horribly wrong.

I would see it in the debriefs we held when we got back and the fat Master Sergeant was physically present. In the former case, he was someone living vicariously through those of us who actually left the wire and went out on patrols. In the latter case, he was someone who felt that he had no greater opportunity for success in his career than catching a soldier making a mistake under the most trying of circumstances. In both cases, I would argue that they were the products of failed leadership.

All of us saw the same recruiting videos. All of us, when we started out, wanted to be that cool camouflaged ninja jumping out of planes, shooting big guns, and blowing stuff up only to magically reappear moments later wearing a fancy dress uniform surrounded by our adoring fellow Americans. Those fat Master Sergeants started out the exact same way. They wanted to be part of something bigger than themselves. Like all of us, they wanted to be part of something special. They wanted to be part of something elite. Which leads quite naturally to step two of Sergeant Nolan's Leadership Model, which is set a standard of excellence.

You see, those of us who join the military quite literally join a priesthood. Just like any other priesthood we wear different clothes, we abide by stricter rules than the greater society of which we are a part, and most importantly we sacrifice much of our personal lives in service to the greater good. Our vocation is sacred and those of us who take our oaths of service and duty with a sense of spiritual obligation do not tolerate the presence of those who profane our community by treating it like it's just some other job. To be a leader among warriors, you must actually enforce a standard of excellence – that's step three in the model for those of you I haven't put to sleep yet – both for yourself as well as for those put within your charge. Let me say that again. To be a leader among warriors, you must actually enforce a standard of excellence both for yourself and for those put within your charge. Failure to do so will be viewed as a violation of the faith, a violation of the contract that we, as members of the brotherhood of arms, have with each other.

I don't want to take up too much more of everyone's time, but I do want to put my comments in some context because my observations of leadership can be taken to an extreme. My model of leadership is harsh because war is violence en masse and violence is governed by immutable laws of nature. But I think we have all seen that superior whose ambition is unquenchable. Quite often they are amazing people. They are among the best – which is step one of my model, right? And they demand a lot from their men, quite often too much – but isn't that just setting a standard of excellence – step two? And such leaders often rule with an iron will and a complete intolerance for dissension. Isn't that just enforcing the standard? Yes, it is. So clearly my model is missing something.

I will tell you that I am proud to serve in the U.S. military for one reason more than any other. Having traveled the world, I can tell you that no other country on Earth is as capable of forgiveness and compassion as we are. Sure, in some countries the people walking the streets may be a bit more friendly. We, Americans, have an extremely high work ethic that often appears as a disregard for others when in fact we are simply very busy going about, well, our business! But other countries that never even experienced the kind of attack we did in Pearl Harbor, have never forgiven the Japanese to this very day. In America, we eat sushi, watch anime, and couldn't even imagine a world without Mr. Miyagi. We, as a nation, quite literally love the Japanese. That, ladies and gentlemen, is not normal.

On September 11th, 2001, our country was attacked by a group of militant fundamentalist Muslims. Two wars followed and the violence rages on to this very day. And yet I will give my life in the defense of Islam and the right of my fellow Muslim countrymen to worship as they see fit. Compared to the Sunnis and Shi'ites in other parts of the world who have been fighting each other for hundreds of years - that is not normal.

We, Americans, however, are great exactly because of this

compassion for humanity. And as long as you keep such compassion front and center of your motivation, you will be rightly guided in your actions, whether that involves following Sergeant Nolan's leadership model or anything else you might engage in during your time in our profession of arms. And so it is, gentlemen, I say to you congratulations and good luck in your future endeavors. Thank you, ladies and gentlemen, for your time. General Williams, sir, good afternoon.

The Effects of Exposure

For those who have not been called, it is difficult to understand the extent to which fighting gets in the blood of those of us whose vocation is the profession of arms. Actual warriors, try as they may, are incapable of resisting the sirens' call and will spend their entire lives, one way or another, involved in the profession. The profession of arms is not just a job; it truly is a way of life. It is a way of life characterized by the search for a perfection of self that must include both absolute compassion for self and others as well as a completely unforgiving dedication to discipline and responsibility.

Tokitsu does a very good job of explaining how, in the Asian world, Confucianism, and its emphasis on ritual, led to the evolution of kata within the oriental martial arts and how these combat rituals embody as well as enhance the personal attributes highly prized by Confucianism.[10] Similarly, the military traditions and ceremonies practiced by military organizations all over the world both enhance and display the results of the individual self-discipline of each warrior in its contribution to the group as a whole. So, just as the individual martial artist practices his or her form, in modern warfighting, the individual warrior focuses on practicing his or her marksmanship skills that require the application and development of a set of very precise movements and stances (personal ritual) just like the ancient forms of oriental martial arts. The military organization practices drill and ceremonies to exercise the combining of individuals into one organism that likewise practices its rituals of self-discipline. The more self-discipline a military unit has, the more it will fight as a single organism in combat. Thus, making it impervious to any sort of divide and conquer strategy an enemy might try to employ. Since a military unit's self-discipline is equal to the sum of the self-discipline of the individual warriors that comprise that unit, the important thing remains the self-discipline of the individual.

Acceptance of one's vocation into the brotherhood of arms is necessary and has real consequences for the ability of the individual service member to maximize their impact on the world. Serving in the combat arms of any military can be horrible at times. There is nothing truly fun about the worst of it because, at the most basic level, a warrior training for combat must engage in the conditioning that develops the ability to sustain damage. This is done by exposing the warrior to the elements of nature. It is done by beating him with a medicine ball. It is done by subjecting him to significant and sustained amounts of endurance training. It is done by utilizing any number of unpleasant training techniques. The military even has a way at times of making things that should be fun, like rappelling out of a helicopter or shooting very large machine guns, a completely non-enjoyable experience. This is understandable. Military organizations are not there to have fun. They exist to fight and destroy the enemies of their nation who are equally dedicated to destroying them.

In order for any of these techniques to produce the maximum benefit, not only must the subjected warrior be willing to cooperate, he must desire to push it to the limit as well. To obtain this level of participation, military leaders have to explain the reasons for the training and the benefits to be gained, because only a fully informed warrior is truly free to make a conscious decision to accept the rigors of what he is about to be subjected to. And only a warrior who has accepted his vocation fully will make that conscious decision wholeheartedly. Otherwise, he will only 'half-ass" his way through it.

That can become a huge problem because a warrior who does not give himself completely to his training establishes a standard of mediocrity. Just one such soldier in a unit can be a temptation to all the other soldiers to slack off. Military leaders, though, must understand the internal struggle the warrior is undergoing and must analyze whether or not the military is truly the vocation of this particular soldier and offer career guidance accordingly. Retaining service members simply for the sake of keeping the ranks filled can be dangerous because an unmotivated attitude can spread like a virus throughout an organization. But the importance of all accepting the call of their vocation goes beyond just organizational morale.

It has long been known that soldiers tend to fight for concern over each other as much, if not more, than any other reason.[11] A cynical person might point out, however, that this concern for one's fellow soldier may still have selfish roots by virtue of the fact that there is safety in numbers. So by protecting my fellow soldiers, I am effectively protecting myself. I have witnessed such a thing among third-world ragtag posses composed of tribesmen whose respective tribes have a temporary alignment of interests. The performance of such bands, once the bullets start flying, can leave much to be desired.

An all-volunteer military filled with warriors who have each individually accepted their vocation is the ideal. Admittedly, this ideal does not exist in significant numbers, but there are small units and guerrilla organizations that come very close. One of the most interesting observations I have had again and again throughout my military career is that a small group of motivated voluntary warriors can easily defeat a significantly larger and far better resourced organization filled with conscripts. This highlights the fact that retaining soldiers simply to fill the ranks ultimately succumbs to the law of diminishing returns. There are only so many people called to serve in the mission of any organization and when the entity grows beyond the limit of that population, performance of necessity will suffer.

And to make matters worse, the stresses of combat wear away at the discipline and resilience of even those truly called to serve. Over time cracks will begin to show. An example of these 'cracks' involves the men of a unit I was serving in that had seen multiple deployments and a fairly high operational tempo, particularly for a reserve component organization. At the time I wrote the message below, Robert Bales, was a soldier stationed in Afghanistan, had recently left his base in the Panjwai District near Kandahar and killed seventeen civilians while they slept, nine of them children, burned many of the bodies, and committed other criminal acts on the evening of March 11, 2012. Neither I nor my intended audience at the time knew most of the details of the incident. All we knew was that a soldier had killed a bunch of civilians overnight on his own accord. Much to my surprise, many of my fellow soldiers were somewhat sympathetic towards this individual and were posting various comments on social media platforms along the lines of, 'those Afghans probably had it coming,' and other similar comments. I realized that my soldiers were starting to show signs of stress from their own multiple deployments in support of the war on terror and so I wrote this message to them primarily with the intention of mentally shoring up the ranks and maintaining discipline in the short-term.

* * *

To my Brothers-in-Arms,

Recently an American soldier left his base in Afghanistan and proceeded to kill several Afghan civilians as they slept. I have seen and heard many responses from within our ranks, all of a similar vein, that say something along the lines of, 'although I don't condone what that soldier did, we should not forget what our enemies did on September 11th.' I believe this creates the perfect opportunity to have a frank discussion that is seldom held among our ranks, the ranks of the enlisted service member. To be clear, I cannot emphasize enough that I am NOT speaking to the specific incident cited above, but rather I am merely utilizing what little facts are known about the incident, and there are admittedly few at this point, to highlight an important aspect of our way of life.

We know at this point that the individual involved in the incident was a 38-year-old Staff Sergeant, married, with two children. He has 11 years of service and had already made the sacrifices involved in three previous deployments to Iraq. Also, by all accounts thus far, he was not a substandard performer. Thus, he had clearly accrued unto himself a fair amount of honor and respect, to say the least. I fully recognize all of that. The accrual of such honor, however, like the accrual of tremendous wealth, can be easily squandered.

When a member of our ranks willfully and knowingly takes any such action that, 1) puts the lives of other soldiers needlessly at risk (there was a search party being formed to leave the wire to look for the soldier), 2) flies in the face of the military objectives set by our superior officers, and 3) readily advances the cause of our enemies, that member has, without exaggeration, become an enemy himself. And I am arguing that such a person should be treated accordingly. As members of the brotherhood-of-arms, we are all aware of how complex combat can be and why the draconian discipline that exists within our community serves at once a tactical, operational, and strategic purpose. Although I have always advised my Commanding Officers to show leniency and refrain from utilizing any of the authorities granted to them by the Uniform Code of Military Justice, thereby leaving the nurturing of discipline within the hands of Non-Commissioned Officers, when one of our own acts so egregiously, as this soldier appears to have done in Afghanistan, we have no choice but to remember our oath to defend this

Nation against all enemies, both foreign and domestic, when deciding upon the proper course of action to take.

As a lifelong martial artist, I have been asked on several occasions why Shaolin monks, Buddhists essentially forbidden from willfully killing another person, would dedicate their lives to mastering ancient forms of combat. The answer is that these monks seek to perfect themselves and since warfare destroys all that is impermanent without regard, this particular tradition has found the model of warfare to be the perfect construct within which they find a purifying fire; one that ultimately allows for nothing to survive of the self beyond that which is immortal.

Because warfare itself is absolutely unforgiving, our warrior culture is unforgiving. Although failure and defeat are accepted when they happen, they are not tolerated. Our entire military community has worked very hard to create an enterprise-wide learning environment where appropriate corrective actions are identified and implemented as swiftly as possible in response to failure. It takes discipline to do this, and it is exactly because of our high level of discipline, that our military ranks first in the world.

So it is, my brothers, that I must urge you, when faced with the commission of war crimes by one of our own, to look upon such a newly minted enemy with unforgiving eyes and calloused hearts. Rest assured that I will never forget what our enemies have done. But know that it is exactly because our enemies are merciless, that we must be merciless with ourselves in preparation for the fields of battle.

* * *

But such harsh words spoken out of necessity are of limited value. They may work for a short while, but the fact remains that the audience was comprised of good men who never once waivered from wanting to do good things. It was incumbent upon these men, their leadership, and their country to understand that some limits were being reached. It was time for compassion.

There is a very common human tendency to often think that if some is good, then more is better. It is easy to see the error of this when speaking of generalities from which we are removed, but it is a very different thing when we are living in the moment and involved with things that have personal value to us. As warriors, we have a natural tendency to lean towards discipline and the harsh criticism of self. It is completely understandable; however, just because some is good does not mean that more is better. As much as we must apply a sense of personal responsibility to self and others at all times, we must also and equally apply a sense of compassion to self and others or the imbalance in time will lead to defeat, one way or another. As warriors we must tread the middle way.

Chapter Notes

[10] Tokitsu, Kenji. (2010). *The Katas: The Meaning behind the Movements*. Rochester, VT: Inner Traditions.

[11] Leonard Wong, Thomas A. Kolditz, Raymond A. Millen, & Terrence M. Potter. *Why They Fight: Combat Motivation in the Iraq War*. Strategic Studies Institute, U.S. Army War

College. July 2003.

About the Author

Michael E. Nolan is a retired Staff Sergeant who served as an infantryman in the Marine Corps, Marine Corps Reserves, and the Army National Guard between the years 1990 to 2016. During his military service he participated in Operation Desert Shield/Desert Storm, Operation Provide Promise/Deny Flight, and United Nations Operation Somalia with 1st Battalion, 8th Marines. With the 3rd Battalion, 25th Marines he participated in Joint Task Force Six along the U.S.-Mexican border. He also did two tours in Iraq, first with the 1452nd Transportation Company in support of Operation Iraqi Freedom 04-05, and then with the 3rd Battalion, 116th Infantry Brigade Combat Team in support of Operation Iraqi Freedom 07-08. His military decorations include the Legion of Merit, Bronze Star Medal, Meritorious Service Medal, Army Achievement Medal (3 awards), Army Reserve Component Achievement Medal (7 awards), and the Combat Infantryman's Badge among others.

Michael graduated magna cum laude in 1998 with a Bachelor of Science degree in Business Administration from Franklin University. He also holds a Master of Business Administration degree (2006) from the University of Phoenix as well as a Master of Science degree in National Resource Strategy (2013) from The Eisenhower School at National Defense University where Michael was an Afghanistan/Pakistan Fellow and a member of the Land Combat Systems industry study. He also has twenty years of civilian service in both the defense and intelligence arenas that included roles as the Chief

Financial Officer for the standup of the Defense POW/MIA Accounting Agency as well as working as a Senior Advisor to the Ministry of Defense of the Government of the Islamic Republic of Afghanistan.

Michael is a lifelong martial artist having studied various arts from all over the world but focusing his efforts primarily on the Chinese martial arts. He studied Wing Chun (Yong Chun) and Tai Chi from Dr. Fred Ming-An Wu starting in 1983 until his death in 2000, excepting periods of military service. Currently, Michael studies Shuai Chiao in Northern Virginia under Master Nick Masi, a student of Dr. Daniel Chi-hsiu Weng, himself a top disciple of the world-renowned Grandmaster Chang Tung-Sheng. Otherwise, Michael enjoys spending time with his beautiful wife, Erin, and his two daughters, or hanging out in the woods enjoying nature.

If you would like to reach out to the author, please go to the following website and use the contact form:

www.mikenovembermedia.com

Printed in Great Britain
by Amazon